The Mechanic, My Car and Other Things

Erin Kate

BookLeaf Publishing

The Mechanic, My Car and Other Things ©
2022 Erin Kate

Presentation by *BookLeaf Publishing*

Web: www.bookleafpub.com

E-mail: info@bookleafpub.com

ISBN: 9789395756945

First edition 2022

DEDICATION

for trent

your favourite customer

for once in your life it's quiet as the curtain
closes on the first act
the radio announcer prescribes tennessee
whiskey for your pain
wise men say if your first love dies young, you
shouldn't look back
even wiser men fuck the second until they forget
the first one's name

how lucky am i to have held your audience for
even an instant
you are an entire galaxy tied together with
crystalline green eyes
your ship steady and sure against my torrents of
resistance
glasses of endless refusals and bottles of never
knowing why

so many nights i spent wanting you and days i
spent taunting you
if you'd brushed my skin with your fingertips
you'd have felt the spark
i am destined to be canonised the patron saint of
being blue
but i love you so much my bones strain under
the weight of my heart

how beautiful it is to share
the silence

i want the quiet comfort of a boring life
to complain about the way you make the bed
i want the honour and pride of the second wife
to pull from your back the first one's knife
i want to watch you work on your car in the shed
to wash up your favourite mug in the mornings
i want to bask in the hope of what lies ahead
to keep you close despite the psychic warnings
to dream about the speeches and vows to be said
to hope that for you, having had to marry twice
that the second time around will surely suffice.

this one is different because it's us

the desperate wanting of nights spent apart
i'm nothing special, just a lonely heart
aching only to beat in time with your own
the latent longing and whispers in the dark

the hungry stare that turns you to stone
the tenderness that cuts to the bone
from everything i've ever tasted of love
i choose every time to work alone

until you and i work hand in glove
an angel sent from heaven above
built from scratch just for little jolene
we found a love i couldn't dream of

cornflower blue and seafoam green
a couple months sober and finally clean
a daydream i've had since i was sixteen
twin golden thrones for a king and a queen

completely and perfectly and incandescently happy

i could stay like this forever
i found god in the taste of your lips
our bodies and souls twisted together
on all fours with your hands on my hips

they'll cut off your hands for stealing my heart
your mouth on mine makes the motions feel like
art
the final throes of our dance are my favourite
part
your sigh is a gospel and i whisper amen

the month of august belongs to us
we can forget the world for a little while
we make a mess and i make a fuss
about the ruined sheets with a cheeky smile

we make the best of a bad situation
turn the pain into simultaneous elation
and it's worth the neighbourhood reputation
to worship at your temple again and again

spoiler alert: it's always been you

The kitchen clock reads a quarter to four
It's never enough, you'll always want more
The stupid shit I wrote
One hand around my throat
The other reaching for the cutlery drawer

Never before was a circle so vicious
I'd never laid eyes a man so ambitious
An itch you can't scratch
A bitch you can't catch
But crossing the line still feels so delicious

I'd move the coffee table so we could dance
But I know even now we'll never have a chance
Two bottles of wine
We've run out of time
Now you know why they call it a bad romance

My heart is a mosaic of shattered glass
I'm foolish and broken and stuck in the past
Look into my eyes
A hundred goodbyes
Our attempts at forever would crumble so fast

I'm a street cordoned off, a red traffic light
Tyres scream like sirens in the middle of the
night
I slam on the brakes
All I see is your face
Do you think that one day it'll all be alright?

My tongue is a cherry stem tied in a knot
I'm tipped over and poured out like a little
teapot
Holding back tears
I've been dead for years
Can't you see I'm waiting for you to take a shot?

I'm sick to death of these shitty Mondays
You make me want you in a hundred different
ways
I'll give you a call
I'll give you my all
But would it ever be enough for you to want to
stay?

Shipwrecked in my head with no sign of dry
land
You calm the storm with the touch of your hand
My heartbeat gets faster
You're a natural disaster

I'm stuck in your orbit and sunk in your
quicksand

It takes all of my courage to pick up the phone
I sit there for hours listening to the tone
I search for a clue
I find nothing new
So in synchrony forever we'll both be alone

You play on my mind til I feel that same ache
It's late and I want you and I'm wide awake
I'll pretend to hate it
But I think you could make it
Like a nine point five Richter scale earthquake

I know for sure there's a god up there
I see him when your hands are tangled in my
hair
The world at our feet
Just friends between sheets
I'd hate you to think that I actually care

I try to keep score but your cards have me beat
Too good at this game so you must be a cheat
Bracelets of leather
You're saying forever
But I don't want to stay if I have to compete

Take my hand in yours and promise me this

I don't want you to be just another I miss
Quiet my fears
Lay with me here
Tell me you only want one more first kiss

We're laughing in the car at some stupid joke
You wind down the window and buy me a coke
You're sweet just like honey
You're not fucking funny
Still you're stuck to me like stale cigarette
smoke

i think there's a reason it
rhymes with satanic

afternoon car ride
two pairs of eyes wide
he says no chance I'd
ever leave your side

our back and forth style
concurrent exile
your cheshire cat smile
hope you'll stay a while

another near miss
love's tangible bliss
lust's poisonous kiss
no i don't want this

twisted and manic
passion volcanic
down like titanic
fucking mechanic

the dulcet tones of throwing up in the kitchen sink around four o'clock on a tuesday morning in suburbia

a girl your age is a homewrecking whore
when playing with your dolls becomes such a
bore
beating yourself up becomes another chore
doesn't matter if you're up until half past four
picking up pieces of your heart off the floor
you're untouched and unfucked but you're
rotten to the core

small and saccharine sweet is she
i wish i wasn't this kind of twenty three
the boys say nothing good comes for free
they always ask what the fuck is wrong with me
if the angels could hear my strained midnight
plea
they'd say it's right in front of me and i still
can't see

maybe im full of it but you're full of tattoos
your mercurial greens and my guarded blues
a matching set of air signs with so much to lose

constantly off balance and missing our cues
both of us searching in bottles of booze
im not yours to keep but you still can't refuse

a girl my age only wants a game to play
girls like me never mean what they say
im completely full of shit but im perfectly okay
if you ever packed yourself up and walked away
you know my drunken heart would beg for you
to stay
but I'd hush her and pour another drink either
way

a joke without a punchline

Two people are wandering through an auto parts shop at nine o'clock on a Saturday morning and one turns to the other and says hey, I can't fucking breathe. It hurts when I think about you and it hurts when I don't. I'm sick to my fucking stomach from the moment I wake up until the moment I fall asleep. You're the devil. Do you know that? You're the fucking devil. But you're my salvation and the sound of your laugh is the purest sound in the world.

love or something like it

i loved you long before i could ever touch you
i ached for all the lives we lived in my head
i tried so hard not to be the one to rush you
i just wanted to feel you next to me in bed
to watch the blood rush red under your ivory
skin
to see pink and soft become puffy and swollen
you were pale white before i coloured you in
i was bruised blue before you coloured me
golden

i hope you still think of me
and i hope it hurts

how on earth could any old lovesick fool
ever have a hope in hell of getting over you
the cigarette smoke that will always linger
the pale against the tan on my left ring finger
maybe i could never hold you tight enough
for you to want to stay when things got rough
and now you stick in my throat like a bitter pill
and im bleeding all alone in the home we built
thinking of may and your suit and my white
dress
i just really thought you'd always love me the
best
but enjoy your second shot at everlasting
romance
the guilt will kill you long before i ever get a
chance

i don't want to miss a single moment

i don't think i've ever been in love, not really
the feeling in my chest is entirely foreign to me
whatever came first was only habit or proximity
but that was all before this perfect fantasy

in our world we can live a hundred lives
we can build our home in the afterglow
in our world there are no ex-wives
no broken hearts or tales of woe

and now we can make a new tradition
you pull at my strings like a gifted musician
im on my knees for the act of contrition
for the moments we took without permission

i've long given up those terrible choices
now we don't have to hide or sleep alone
we whisper into the phone in hushed voices
get your clothes off, i'm coming home

it starts with a busted commodore - stop me if you've heard this one before

i could've been anybody
i could've been nobody, true
but i could've been somebody too
could've been a lot of things, see
and later on i would be

but for now i was sat amongst all of the guys
thinking how sick i was of all of the lies
thinking about the way the sunlight hit your eyes
and i wondered if you were thinking the same as me
angry for no reason over number nineteen
because halsey was robbed and so was amy
but you probably didn't think the same of cardi b
i had given that old dance so many tries

And Nietzsche says that God is dead, but as I
watched the way you worked, watched your
hands, I don't know how he could ever have
been so certain.

i would sit there in your chair thinking holy shit

knowing that there was nothing holy about it
all the shit we went through
all the shit I wanted to do
those bittersweet daydreams that made me sick

There were never enough hours, could never
have been enough hours in any weekend so we
spilled over into the workdays. It was ethereal,
electric, effortless, the way it feels when the last
piece of the puzzle at long last falls into place.
We were strangers, and then we weren't, and
somehow painfully slowly yet all at once you
had gone from a question mark, an unknown
quantity, a name without a face, to somebody I
knew inside out, couldn't live without, a home
base.

then i'd get stuck in that same twisted dream
every night
devils snare wrapped around my ribcage
squeezing tight
wake up breathless without you to say i'm here,
it's alright
the ceiling fan circling its midnight dance was
the saddest sight

and thank god thank god THANK GOD for
august and everything after
          everything before was a fucking disaster

i can still see the candlelight flicker on your face
as we sat together watching the world fall apart
i thought that maybe i needed space
or some extra time to find my place
but i just wanted to break my own heart
the gentle rap of your knuckles on the door
the blurring of lines like impressionist art
the sound of your belt buckle hitting the floor
it was finally finally finally the start

say what you will but your belt looks good on
my bedpost
and your name tastes good in my mouth
and the pain is a sweet little memento
of the shivers as your hands travelled south

listen closely, can you hear the bells?
i swear to god i could see everything right there
even the tiny socks and the teddy bears
i kept that poker face fixed in place
but you already knew all of my tells

i want your sunday night whispers in the dark
i want your monday morning moods
i want your lazy saturdays in the park
i want your friday afternoons
i want the secrets you keep under your skin
i want the words you held back so i could win

i want the photographs you hide in the biscuit tin
i want to give you the courage to face your fears
and it would be okay even if you came dead last
each time
because i'd still be there waiting for you at the
finish line
even if reaching the sky took us fifty years
the luckiest girl and the finest story ever told
that of all of the hands in the world you could
hold
you picked mine

forever (n.) for all future time; for always. (oxford dictionary)

You're mine and there's nothing I wouldn't do to hold onto this forever. You were the catalyst for everything. You were the one who told me not to be so scared.

I laid awake at night staring at the ceiling,
cuddled up next to my sin and my guilt
Your spirit shattered my pride
Your honour saw through my lies
Your smile cleared up my grey skies
The universe was laying the brick and the mortar
long before we realised something was being
built.

It was too hard to tell you no
Or to tell you to go
I knew that I should
But I knew that I would
Take you any way that I could

And I kept thinking it had to end but it never did
it was late June

and far too soon
but I stared at the moon
and wondered about the starry sky behind your
eyelids.

In July I looked in the mirror and I thought to
myself,
       You fought
       But you were caught
       And you just knew
       He could have you
       Any way he wanted to
Because you were always my favourite book on
the shelf.

And then it was mid-August and it had been
ordained that you'd be the architect of future
days. We sit up late at night painting the walls
with our plans. We fuck until we see stars and
you tell me about your cars and I tell you about
my scars and I find peace in the way your voice
sounds with my head against your shoulder.

And I know you're waiting for me to give you
something to keep
       to tell you something real
       to tell you how I feel
Never knowing that I tell you every night before
I go to sleep.

Your head is heavy on my chest and I whisper
into the dark,

"I love you. I'm in love with you. Please don't
go."

When you leave in the morning I can feel the
flesh tear, as if our skin had grown together
overnight.

The wrench in my stomach as I'm watching your
taillights disappear
like muscle tearing from bone
waiting for you to light up my phone
waiting to hear that you're coming home
for the butterflies in my stomach while I wait for
the headlights to tell me you're here.

I want to keep a picture of you on the dash for
the nights when I'm driving too fast so I can look
at you right before the crash and know you'll
always be my last.

I found religion in the colour of your eyes
the sound of your laugh
and the warmth of your skin.

This is the body of Christ

this is the word of the Lord
this is the original sin.

I worship at your church
I whisper your prayer
Forever and ever, amen.

It's almost Halloween now and everyone else
can be anything they want but I'm going to be
yours every year.

alice

we fucked until we'd had our fill
chest to chest and skin to skin
and all the times i'd said i never will
to think that you could love me still
though god's hands tremble with our sin
the golden light flowing through each vein
your head resting under my chin
the sanctity of delicious pain
you look up at me with your cheshire cat grin
a feeling time could never kill

hello, you

it's my old favourite guns n roses shirt
it's the pair of blue levis that fit just right
it's my converse with just the right touch of dirt
it's coming home together at the end of the night

it's worn in perfect like an old leather jacket
it's the sideways look of a shared inside joke
it's you always saying 'i'm going to sack it'
it's the solace of a swill of jack daniels and coke

it's the calendar flipping to six months past
it's searching for signs in every song
it's the letters to you that stayed in the drafts
it's realising it was you all along

rapunzel, rapunzel, let down your hair

lay awake all night staring up at the ceiling
punchdrunk and wired and hooked on a feeling
you wanna get there fast so you can take it slow
don't go

not half as happy as you thought your wife
would make you
the opposite of where you thought your life
would take you
but this one is cotton candy and she could eat
you whole
don't go

spends her weekends crying for you on the
bathroom floor
makes you wanna say i'm right here, you
miserable whore
she goes to him and you taste bile in your throat
don't go

you thought love was blue but it's evergreen
yet you spend months living in the space
between

ask the stars if she'll be yours but they don't
know
don't go

farmers spend months waiting for the rain
i spent my whole week waiting for saturday
now i spend all day waiting for you to get home
i fill entire books with love letters and prose
and i love you more than you will ever know
don't go

plans

there'll be storybooks
little hats and socks
other tiny things
a diamond ring
(perhaps wishful thinking)
objects with a purpose i don't yet understand
something we made with our happy hands
our happy glands
and you'll hold me carefully
lest you interrupt our little group of cells
multiplying into something great
i'm not really interested in anything
that's not taking me closer to that.

what if it never goes away?

i look back and wonder if i could ever have
known
how your callous indifference would cut to the
bone
i promise i'm trying to be okay on my own
but it's me again, please don't hang up the phone

in sickness and in health
for better or for worse
the hand we were dealt
forever is a curse

and you were a no-show
our marriage in a coffin
but those old wedding photos
i still look at them often

i stand alone in the shed trying to feel you here
i stand in line at the store trying to hold back
tears
i study your horoscope trying to make things
clear
all i see now is your taillights as they disappear

lillith and the husband she stole

i can hear her out there in the front yard
teasing and taking up my husband's time
coquettish and brazen in her favourite crime
the perfect life and stepford wife she tore apart

you think it's gonna last with someone that age?
you must think i'm stupid but i can see it all
you're lovestruck by cupid and i'm watching you
fall
i hear her tawdry talons twisting in your ribcage

she will be the last wire that snaps in my head
no use trying anymore so cheers to nine years
i'll be fine on my own with my tears and my
beers
while you whisper sweet nothings to lillith in
bed

i hope you still think of me
and i hope it hurts

how on earth could any old lovesick fool
ever have a hope in hell of getting over you
the cigarette smoke that will always linger
the pale against the tan on my left ring finger
maybe i could never hold you tight enough
for you to want to stay when things got rough
and now you stick in my throat like a bitter pill
and im bleeding all alone in the home we built
thinking of may and your suit and my white
dress
i just really thought you'd always love me the
best
but enjoy your second shot at everlasting
romance
the guilt will kill you long before i ever get a
chance

convalescence

i close my eyes and i count my breathing
in for two and out for four
pick myself up off the floor
darling, don't look at me that way
i just wanted you to want to stay
but i can see you're toying with the thought of
leaving

you get so alone that you get stuck in your brain
your demons with their red hair
your boxes marked handle with care
you want calm but you need a storm
you need a fire to keep you warm
you want the cruel beauty of being in so much
pain

what if you and i keep hurting each other forever
our wounds will weep slowly
our scars are sick trophies
wake breathless in the night
you can give in, it's alright
but i will keep trying every day to make it better